8 Money Mistakes to Avoid at All Costs

Kimberly Carlton, MBA

DEDICATION

For Nika

CONTENTS

WELCOME!

If you won a $1 million lottery today, do you think in 5 years you would be richer than today, poorer, or the same?

A. I'd have fun spending the money until it's gone and probably end up at about the same place I am right now.
B. I'd spend it on all the things I've always wanted but couldn't afford. I prefer to live for today and let tomorrow take care of itself.
C. I'd make a plan first for how much to spend now and how much to put aside for the future, and then learn everything I could about investing.

While I hope you chose C, that isn't how most lottery wins end up. "About 55% of lottery winners go bankrupt. The problem is the people who go bankrupt don't know how to handle the large sum of money. They go on spending sprees, don't pay the taxes and then end up in a bigger financial mess," according to Ask.com. Money problems can't necessarily be solved with more money.

You probably did NOT just win the lottery today, so a more relevant question might be:

Are you tired of feeling like you're on a financial roller-coaster, racing into an unknown future that's out of your control? Well, you're not alone – a lot of people feel overwhelmed by financial pressures these days. If all that dizzying jerking from side to side and forward and back has you reeling, maybe it's time to just jump off the ride. Before you go, grab a harness and parachute so you can hit the ground running, and a map and compass so you know you're running in the right direction.

I know it can be scary, especially if you're not used to managing your own money. Maybe you're just getting started in the world or maybe your spouse has always been the one in charge of the finances, but now circumstances compel you to take a more active role. I'm here to tell you it's not as hard as you think, and you CAN do it. By the end of this Action!Book™, I think you'll be surprised at just how much you're able to do!

(Why is it called an Action!Book™? Because knowing what to do is not the key to financial security, ACTING on that knowledge is. This is a tool to help you do both: wisely choose a course of action, and execute it. The learning comes by doing.)

The problem is that most of us are taught very little about money. It's a sensitive subject, one that many people aren't very willing to discuss in detail openly, yet it's also a critical part of our lives and not something <u>anyone</u> should leave up to someone else. In our society, money is a life necessity no less than food, water, or shelter precisely because those things can hardly be had *without* money. Yet, schools typically don't teach what we need to know about money, parents often hide the truth about money from their kids, and our culture frowns on talking too freely about money in a personal context even as it promotes the virtual worship of the dollar. Is it any surprise people are intimidated?!

Yet for all the myths and jargon that surround the issue, understanding money really is easier than you might think. You do have to get past the "language barrier" – one thing professionals in any field are good at is discouraging average people from participating actively by creating a complicated way of talking about the subject. The harder it seems to understand, the more likely you will be to pay someone else to take care of it for you. Don't get me wrong, there is a place for professional services when it comes to managing your money. But you don't have to sit completely on the sidelines in confusion just because some people like to use fancy words to describe how money works or even because math wasn't your favorite subject in school. Nor do you have to become a financial professional yourself to be able to manage your money well.

The goal of this Action!Book™ is to help you avoid common mistakes and instead to take control over your money, that is to say, take control of your life. I will give you simple, easy-to-understand explanations of how to do that, and these are followed by practical exercises that help you to apply what you just learned to your own personal situation. This is not a theoretical book, nor is it an attempt to explain in detail the theory or philosophy behind effective money management. It is, rather, a practical guide to be <u>used</u> by you as a tool to improve your ability to use your money in the service of your own values and goals.

There's no quick fix here or magic formula for getting rich – I hope by now you know better than to believe in fairy tales. But this <u>is</u> a powerful tool get yourself on solid footing, *if* you apply it. You will need to go beyond reading, and take the time to do the exercises offered and continue to take concrete actions over time to create new habits. If you don't do that, then about the only thing I'd be willing to bet on is that your financial situation one year from now or five years from now will be pretty much the same as it is today (if not worse). If that's OK with you, then do nothing.

If you're ready to embark on a journey in a new direction, though, this is a great place to start! And today is the perfect day to do it! Look back at the past, whatever failures or fears may be there, and say, "*Bon Voyage!*" Let's go!

MISTAKE #1: NOT BEING CLEAR ABOUT WHAT YOU WANT

"If you do not know where you are going, any road will take you there." Lewis Carroll

<u>Why it's important</u>: Setting goals requires you to get clear and specific about what you want. Not doing this is perhaps the most common mistake people make in managing their money. Would you set out on a trip that uses all of your vacation time and savings without first deciding where you want to go and what you want to get out of it? Lewis Carroll said that if you don't know where you're going, any road will get you there. When it comes to your money, that approach can lead you to bankruptcy and even poverty quite easily, and it's very *unlikely* to lead you to security, let alone prosperity.

When you take the time to set goals, you connect your desires to the reasons why they are important to you. How likely are you to continue to pursue something without a clear and compelling reason to do it? Life is busy for most people and there are lots of distractions, so to succeed you need to be very clear about what you want and why it's important to you.

ഇരു

When you set goals, you connect your desires to the reasons why they are important to you.

ഇരു

<u>How to fix it</u>: Setting goals is simply deciding what you want and why. The most useful goals are SMART goals: **<u>S</u>**pecific, **<u>M</u>**easurable, **<u>A</u>**ttainable, **<u>R</u>**elevant, **<u>T</u>**ime-bound. *Specific* means clear and well defined. *Measurable* means there's a way to know if the goal has been achieved or not. *Attainable* means the goal is realistic and can be achieved with the resources – time, skills, etc. – that you have or can get. *Relevant* means the goal will bring you closer to where you want to be. *Time-bound* means there's a deadline for when the goal will be achieved.

The most powerful way to write goals is to use the present or past tense and describe what will be true when the goal is accomplished. In this way, "I want to earn a million dollars this year" becomes "I earn a million dollars a year" or "I earned a million dollars this year."

> **SMART Goals**
>
> **S** = Specific
> **M** = Measurable
> **A** = Attainable
> **R** = Relevant
> **T** = Time-bound

Read the following three goals and decide whether they are SMART goals:

1. I have more than $10,000 in my bank account on December 31, 2010.
2. I will have enough money to travel whenever I feel like it.
3. I have all my credit cards paid off before next Christmas.

Goal #1 meets the criteria because it states exactly what will be accomplished (specific), you can tell whether it's been achieved by comparing an actual bank balance on a specific date to the amount desired (measurable), it can be done (attainable), it reflects control over your money (relevant) and there's a deadline (time-bound). Goal #2, on the other hand, is vague (not specific) because it's unclear how much money is "enough" – travel to where, and how often? Similarly, there is no clear way to know if the goal has been achieved (not measurable), whether it can be done (attainable) or by when (not time-bound). Goal #3 falls somewhere in the middle because it is easy to evaluate whether it has been accomplished (measurable by whether the debt is paid off or not), relevant and time-bound, but it could be improved by defining exactly how much money is needed for the payoff so that it's easier to see what it will take to achieve it (is it attainable?).

Now make it personal: Consider the following questions and record your answers in the space provided. Our focus in this section is on the big picture so we're only looking at long-term goals for now. You'll set your short-term goals later.

How would you rephrase Goal #2 above so it meets the SMART goal criteria?

> *Tip: Keep a Prosperity Notebook to record your answers to the exercises for each Step so that you can more easily see how they all fit together.*

Imagine that 5 years have passed from this day and you have succeeded in taking control of your money. List the 3-5 most important things that have changed for the better. (Examples: I've gotten out of debt; I'm no longer living paycheck to paycheck)

1.
2.
3.
4.
5.

> *Tip: Use positive language, focusing on what you DO want and avoid expressions of what you DON'T want.*

Now re-write the 3-5 statements above in the format of SMART goals. (Example: As of 12/31/2017 all of my credit cards and car loans are paid off and I pay the full balances for new charges on my credit cards every month)

1.
2.
3.
4.
5.

Tip: Remember, SMART goals are
S = Specific
M = Measurable
A = Attainable
R = Relevant
T = Time-bound

Re-read each of your SMART goals and make sure they are **S**pecific, **M**easurable, **A**ttainable, **R**elevant, **T**ime-bound.

Why did you choose these particular goals? What is it about each goal that inspires you?

Close your eyes for 30 seconds and imagine that day in 5 years when you have achieved all your goals. Imagine it fully, in the most vivid detail possible. How do you <u>feel</u> about yourself and your life?

Tip: Write your answer in the PRESENT tense, and incorporate impressions from as many of your five senses as possible. This will make the experience much more <u>real</u> for you!

MISTAKE #2: THINKING MONEY HAS VALUE WITHOUT VALUES

<u>**Why it's important**</u>: We rarely talk about our money as being an extension of ourselves, yet thinking about it this way puts you in a position of power in relation to your money. If you allow money to control you, then your life feels like a constant struggle. When you feel in control of your money, it serves you and helps you experience life in a richly fulfilling way. When you see your money as a force acting in the world on your behalf, it's easier to make choices that support your goals. You realize that the decision to buy something or not is really a choice about who you are and what you value – so turning down a stylish new pair of shoes in favor of more financial security for your family doesn't leave you feeling deprived. It's an easy choice when you know clearly what's important to you and why.

Your money is like an ambassador that represents your values and interests to the world on your behalf.

<u>**How to fix it**</u>: Spending reflects values and how you choose to use your money is one of the most powerful ways you show the world, your family and friends, and even *yourself* what's important to you. That's why we say, "Put your money where your mouth is," when we want to know what someone <u>really</u> believes in. You can be pretty sure that when someone is unwilling to back up their words with their hard-earned cash, they're not as seriously committed to what they're saying as it might otherwise seem.

In her book, *The Soul of Money*, author Lynne Twist makes the point that our beliefs, not only about money but also about how the world works, affect how we <u>use</u> our money. Whether you see money as a force for good or evil in the world, you'll tend to use it that way. In that sense, your money is a sort of ambassador that goes out into the world on your behalf and represents your values and interests. Are you aware and in control of what your money is saying about you?

Many people think their spending decisions are private and that money is separate from morals. Nothing could be further from the truth. Money is perhaps the most powerful means we have of expressing our values and, like it or not, most of us make judgments about others based on how they both get and spend money. "It's just business," is a common justification for what are frequently selfish choices and we all know it, at least when we see it in others. Look at yourself from this same perspective, and make choices consistent with your values.

Now make it personal: Consider the following questions and record your answers in the space provided.

What do you want people to know about you based on how you spend your money?

1.
2.
3.

What was the last purchase you made that you felt really good about, both at the time and after the fact? Why did you feel this way?

Tip: To gain a deeper understanding, ask "why" several times.
For example: I was happy because I've wanted it for a long time. Why? Because I saw it on Oprah. Why does that matter? Because I admire her. Why? Because she helps others make their lives better. Oh, so you were happy because it felt good to see yourself as being similar to someone you admire for their generosity. Now I see!

When have you purchased something that you later regretted? Why did you regret it?

Which experience is more normal for you – feeling great about your purchase decisions, or feeling regret? Why?

What values are most important to you, and why? How do your current spending habits reflect these values?

My Top Values	Why It Matters to Me	Because I have this value, I spend money on:

If you were determined to spend your money only on those things that you consider a reflection of your values, in what ways would your spending behavior change? What might you stop doing or buying? What might you do more of?

MISTAKE #3: COMPARING OURSELVES – BUT ONLY TO THOSE BETTER OFF

Why it's important: Unless you know your own definition of wealth, you risk wasting your time and life working to acquire things that other people think you should want or need while possibly neglecting to acquire and appreciate what YOU truly value. It's all too easy to get caught up in "keeping up with the Joneses" and, since there will <u>always</u> be someone who has more than you do, you can get stuck on a never-ending treadmill that leaves you exhausted and takes you nowhere. If you take the time to decide for
 yourself what you need to feel secure, not only are you more likely to get it but you are also much more likely to feel satisfied and grateful for the wealth you DO have.

If you are living in the United States, regardless of your income level, you ARE wealthy already by the standards of the majority of people alive in the world today. If you're like most people and only compare yourself to those who have <u>more</u> than you, rather than those who have <u>less</u> than you, this reality may be hard for you to see and appreciate. The danger here is that if your comparisons always leave you feeling like the loser, you will find it very difficult to reach your financial goals because you may be too demoralized to even make the effort and you'll probably set yourself up – again – to lose by setting unrealistic goals in the first place. This is why it's important to look at where you are now in terms of *both* positive *and* negative comparisons.

Whether or not you are "wealthy" depends on how you look at it – based on what you choose as a point of comparison, and based on how much is enough to satisfy your current needs. For example, at one point in my life I was earning $500 a month and I felt like that was an extravagant salary because it covered all my living expenses with more than enough left over to "play" with. At another point in my life, a salary of $5,000 a month would not have been enough to cover all my living expenses even without spending anything on extras like meals out, entertainment, etc. So wealth is not about any particular number of dollars in your bank account, it's about having enough to meet your needs.

ഇ൪൧

How wealthy you feel depends on who you compare yourself to and how much it takes to satisfy your needs.

ഇ൪൧

How to fix it: A dictionary definition of *wealth* is a large amount of money or an abundance of something. We tend to think of wealth as referring primarily to money or the things that money can buy, and secondarily to having a lot of the things that money can't buy. The key point to understand is that each of us defines wealth somewhat differently – how much is enough? Ultimately the underlying concern we have in common is a desire for security.

It's helpful to remember that money in itself is useless – pieces of paper and metal have value only because we all agree that they do. We use these pieces of metal and paper to acquire the things that do truly have value to us, like food, clothing, shelter, items that give comfort, recreation, etc. How might your definition of wealth change if you thought not about money itself, but instead those things it can buy that give you pleasure or a sense of security? What if you included in your definition the kinds of things that money can't buy?

What does wealth mean to YOU?

 Now make it personal: Consider the following questions and record your answers in the space provided.

What do you need to feel secure? List 3-5 things in each category below. Don't use the word "money," instead list the specific things that you use money to get. You can include a dollar figure that represents the cost per month of buying these things. (Example: Food: $200/mo)

I already have more than enough:	Right now I have just enough:	I would like more:

What is your definition of *wealth*?

Tip: Make this a personal, working definition for YOU. You'll consider yourself wealthy when these conditions are met.

Do you want to be wealthy? Why or why not?

Tip: Consider possible disadvantages. For example, having a lot of money may attract to you people who pretend to be your friend but really just want to use you.

What in your life are you most grateful for? How does this affect your decisions regarding money?

MISTAKE #4: WORKING FOR MONEY

Why it's important: Earned income provides most people with the money they need to live. This requires trading time for money, however, and the amount of time anyone has available to trade for money is obviously limited. This is why wealthy people most often also have passive income and, in fact, focus their energy and intentions on increasing their opportunities to receive passive or residual income. This is called making your money work for you rather than working for your money.

Why do some people, such as entertainers, make so much more money than others, such as teachers? Obviously there are many reasons. What matters here is that entertainers – TV and movie actors, musicians, comedians, etc. – most often work for a while and make recordings of their performances, which are later sold as movies, DVDs, CDs and singles for download on iTunes, etc. In other words, they create a product that can be shared with millions of people for a small fee and they earn residual income from sales that happen long after their work is complete (or, perhaps, they are paid a large up-front fee by someone else who will collect that residual income later). Teachers, on the other hand, are paid for their time and they can only work with a few students at a time.

The ability to earn passive income most often requires the ownership of assets, which we'll get to later. For now, the important point to recognize is that creating passive income streams gives you much greater long-term earning potential than trading time for money does.

There is another meaning to the phrase "working for money" that is important here. We all need money but if you're working for money, then money is the master that controls you. If you're working for yourself, for your dreams, and for the sake of your unique contribution to the world, then money takes its rightful place as compensation for the value your work produces for yourself and others.

How to fix it: You probably already know that income means the money

ᾣ∓

Passive income streams give you much greater earning potential than trading time for money.

ᾣ∓

Income is an inflow of money you receive in compensation for the value you provide to others.

you get from your activities, usually in the form of salary or wages for work. This is what people commonly think of first: <u>earned</u> income. You simply trade a set amount of time (as well as any required skills and expertise you may have) for a specific number of dollars in a series of relatively simple transactions. Normally, the government takes its cut off the top in the form of payroll taxes.

Income represents a flow and is normally measured over a specific period of time, usually one year. For a household it might be measured on your IRS Form 1040, your bank statements, etc. A small business would measure it on its Income Statement, also known as a Profit-and-Loss Statement. Because money flows in and flows out, we talk about income streams to distinguish between different types of income.

A very powerful, though less common, source of income is "<u>passive</u>" or residual income. Unlike earned income, where time is traded for money, passive income continues to flow to you even when you're not working. This is what people often mean when they say, "earn money in your sleep." Passive income is created when you invest in something (called *assets*, see Mistake #7) that pays back over time. Some examples of passive or residual income are: annuities (fixed payments over time, like a retirement plan offers), royalties (payments from ongoing sales of books you've written, songs you've recorded, etc.), and rental income (from real estate or equipment you own that others use for a fee).

&0&3

Passive income is created from investment in assets.

&0&3

One way to think about income is as a reflection, or compensation, for the value you provide to others. If you want to increase your income, then, you need to have a clear understanding of what you have to offer that can benefit other people and that they are willing to pay for. This will usually be one of three things: products (things that you make or purchase for resale), services (something you are skilled at doing for other people), and information (knowledge you have about something that you can share with others).

 Now make it personal: Consider the following questions and record your answers in the space provided or in your Prosperity Notebook.

List all the sources of income you currently have and note whether they are "earned" (i.e., money traded for time) or "passive" (include everything that does NOT represent an exchange of money for time – such as alimony or child support payments, unemployment, rents, royalties, etc.).

Sources of Income	Earned (√)	Passive (√)

List 3 things you could do in the next 30 days that would improve your ability to generate residual income.

1.
2.
3.

Tip: Focus on the <u>actions</u> you could take that would be first steps in this direction. For example, you could learn more about how others have earned passive income.

What do you love to make or do so much that you have become (or could become) very good at it? Consider activities that have been a source of income for you in the past as well as those that have not (for example, a hobby you do just for fun).

Name 3-5 people you know or know about who have made money doing something that you also love to do. Put a star next to the names of the people you know personally (you should have at least one).

Tip: When asking for advice, be as specific as possible. Even people who want to help you may say no if your request is vague or unclear.

    1.

    2.

    3.

    4.

    5.

If you had 30 minutes with the most successful person you named in the previous question, what 3 questions would you ask them?

    1.

    2.

    3.

Now contact the people whose names you put a star next to in the question above and ask them the 3 questions you just wrote. What did you learn?

Tip: NOT asking for help is the surest route to failure. Remember, you miss 100% of the shots you don't take!

Now, find a way to contact the people whose names you did not put a star next to, and ask them the same 3 questions or modified versions of them based on the answers you already received from the people you know.

MISTAKE #5 – THINKING ALL EXPENSES HAVE THE SAME EFFECT ON YOUR BOTTOM LINE

Why it's important: The relationship between your income and expenses defines your financial well-being. For a business, Income – Expenses = Profit (assuming income is greater than expenses; if not, then Income – Expenses = Loss). For households and individuals, we can look at it similarly: Personal Income – Personal Expenses = Personal Profit. Your Personal Profit represents your wealth, and there are only two ways to increase it: increase income and/or reduce expenses.

ഔ൫൙

Personal Income
– Personal Expenses
= Personal Profit

ഔ൫൙

Since discretionary expenses are the only ones that can be easily changed, that is where you need to focus your attention to reduce expenses. When trying to make ends meet, people often focus considerably more energy on trying to reduce expenses than increase income, and this is a mistake! If you are spending more money than you're bringing in, then it certainly makes sense to reduce or even eliminate discretionary expenses where possible, but very few people are successful in the long run at sustaining anything they feel is depriving them of something they truly want and value. This is why *it's essential to focus your efforts on making spending decisions based on your values* (as we explored in Mistake #2) *and finding ways to increase your income* (Mistake #4). After these first two priorities, reducing discretionary expenses would be the third priority – *except* if your monthly expenses are more than your income: if that's the case for you, then reducing discretionary expenses would be your *first* priority (put out the fire first!).

> *Expenses* are outflows of money you spend on what you want or need.

How to fix it: Expenses are income in reverse; outflows of money are normally measured over a set time period like a month or a year. A useful way to look at expenses is to separate them into two broad categories: "fixed" and "discretionary" expenses. From there, they can be further divided into categories like rent, groceries, etc.

Discretionary expenses are those that are relatively easy to change in the short term, while fixed expenses tend to be more stable and require more effort to change. For example, rent (or a mortgage payment) is a fixed expense because it requires regular payments of the same amount and it cannot readily be eliminated or reduced (of course, you can reduce your housing payment by moving into a less expensive place but generally otherwise the amount you pay will not change from month to month). Eliminating a fixed expense usually requires a fairly significant sacrifice at least in terms of effort to change if not lifestyle.

Fixed expenses are harder to reduce than discretionary expenses.

In contrast to fixed expenses, discretionary expenses are those that you do have more immediate control over. One example would be a cable TV bill. It may seem similar to a fixed expense in that the amount you pay is about the same every month and you may pay it automatically, but you have the option of easily changing plans or providers to reduce or increase your level of service and the associated price you pay, and you can eliminate the expense entirely by declining service.

Common household expenses that tend to be fixed are rent or mortgage payments, utilities, car payments, auto insurance, health insurance, groceries and clothing (at least in part) and taxes. Common household discretionary expenses include cable television and Internet service, dining out, entertainment and recreation, travel, and some portion of clothing and grocery expenses (if you buy specialty items or brands). Credit card and other debt payments could be classified as either fixed or discretionary, depending on what you used the borrowed money to acquire. Most credit card debt would be considered discretionary, whereas debt that is used to finance the purchase of assets (e.g., real estate, cars) might better be thought of as a fixed expense.

Keep in mind that expenses, like debt, can have either a positive or negative effect on your long-term well-being. The difference is in what you're spending the money for. We'll cover this in more detail below (Mistake #8) but it boils down to this key question: will this (whatever it is you're buying) help me make more money in the future? If the answer is no, consider whether the expense is really worth it to you.

Credit cards: Almost everyone uses credit cards these days, and credit card debt has become a problem for many people. It's important to recognize that credit card interest and fees can be significant expenses, and carrying large balances on credit cards has a negative effect on your credit score. This can make it very difficult and/or expensive to purchase assets (see Mistake #7), which are critical ingredients for increasing income. For this reason, having control over your credit cards has a ripple effect on your overall financial health.

Here are some things to know about how credit cards affect your credit score:

- Having more than 2 or 3 cards has a negative effect on your score. This includes not only bank-issued cards like Visa, MasterCard, American Express, and Discover, but also store-issued cards (for example, Sears, Target, Bloomingdales, etc.). If you want to improve your credit score, cancel all but the 3 most important credit cards you have, and make sure the company closes your account. Get confirmation in writing.

- Having active cards that you do not use lowers your credit score. If you don't use a card, you can improve your credit score by closing the account.

- Carrying balances above 50% of your total credit limit lowers your score. To improve your credit score, pay your balances down to less than half of your limit for each card.

- Making only the minimum payment on your credit cards hurts your score, and it costs you money in interest charges while taking the longest time to pay off debt. You improve your credit score by paying more than the monthly minimum.

- Paying off your credit card bill in full each month actually hurts your credit score. If you are trying to build up your score, then it might be worthwhile to carry a reasonable balance from month to month, although there is a cost associated with that in interest charges. If your score is above 720 and your goal is to reduce expenses, then pay your balances in full every month.

ଛଠ

Having control over your credit cards has a ripple effect on your financial health.

ଛଠ

 Now make it personal: Consider the following questions and record your answers in the space provided or in your Prosperity Notebook.

Make a list of all your normal monthly expenses, and mark the box that most closely matches the level of importance of each. Put the amount of each expense next to the box you checked <u>and</u> in the total column. Include expenses you pay by cash and credit, and to avoid double-counting do NOT include payments to credit card companies (DO include bank and credit card fees and finance charges, however). When you're done with the list, add the amounts in each column together.

Use the table on the following page. You can download an Excel workbook (Forms) from www.Kimberly-Carlton.com and use it to complete the tables for this Step. Just type in your numbers and the form will automatically calculate the totals for you.

Form 5-1

Expense	Essential (√)	Amount ($)	Nice but not necessary (√)	Amount ($)	Don't really need (√)	Amount ($)	Total ($)
Totals							

Now review the monthly expenses you just entered above, and re-classify them in the table below. Your totals for each line should match the totals for each line in the table above. Add the totals for each column to see how much of your monthly expenses are paid for in cash and how much by credit. Form 5-2:

Expense Category	Amount Paid in Cash	Amount Paid in Credit	Total ($)
Totals			

Evaluate your situation with your credit cards by filling in the table below. Form 5-3:

Name of Card	Current Balance	Avg. Monthly Finance Charge	Average Monthly Payment	Average Monthly Charges
Totals				

How long will it take you to pay off your total balances making your current monthly payments? (Divide your total balance by the total amount you pay each month to find the number of months. For example, a $10,000 total balance divided by $500/mo in payments will take 20 months to repay.)

$$\frac{\text{Total balance}}{\text{Total current payment}} = \text{Number of months}$$

$$\frac{\text{Balance: \$}}{\text{Payment: \$}} = \text{Months:}$$

(or _____ years if you divide the total months by 12)

Now calculate how much you would have to pay each month to pay off the balance in one year (Total balance divided by 12).

$$\frac{\text{Balance: \$}}{12} = \$ \qquad \text{per month}$$

Is this feasible for you?

Tip: If you have balances on several cards, list them in order with the highest interest rates at the top. Pay down balances one at a time, starting with the card having the highest interest rate. After one card is paid off, add the full amount you had been paying to the amount you have been paying on the second most expensive card all along and continue to pay in this way until all cards are paid off.

If not, how much can you pay per month, and how many months will it take you to pay off your debt using that monthly payment? Remember: this assumes your balances *will not grow*, or in other words you will pay this amount PLUS the full amount of all new charges during the month.

$$\frac{\text{Balance: \$}}{\text{Max payment: \$}} = \text{Months to repay in full:}$$

MISTAKE #6 – FAILING TO MEASURE AND TRACK PROGRESS

Why it's important: Focus and discipline are the key benefits a budget provides. Setting clear and specific targets for your spending allows you to focus your attention in a very practical way on your values and priorities, and measuring your actual behavior against your stated intentions supports your ability to successfully achieve your goals. Measuring your progress is the most accurate way to know if you're on the right track or not before you actually arrive at your destination. The only way to measure your progress is to keep track of where your money comes from and where it goes.

When you break it down, a budget really has two parts. One is related to goal-setting, which we discussed earlier, and the other relates to tracking progress, which we'll focus on here. A budget allows you to set specific targets for income and expenses by category, and then to measure actual results against your goals. This is precisely why it can be such a useful, powerful tool. And it's also probably a big part of why so many people find them unpleasant and difficult to use.

Conventional wisdom says that you should create a budget and stick to it if you want to improve your financial situation. This might even work - at least for the most disciplined among us and those who enjoy working with numbers and tracking expenses on a regular basis. For everyone else, though, it's a boring, hateful chore and a constant reminder that we're "a failure" when it comes to managing our money.

Focus and discipline are the key benefits a budget provides.

So if you have the discipline and the desire to make a budget and stick to it, then consider it a useful tool and use it. But if you're someone who would rather suffer a thousand paper cuts on your hands and face than use a budget, the news for you is good too: forget about budgets. Seriously, don't waste your time on something that will only frustrate and discourage you from engaging in the process of actively controlling and owning your money and your relationship with it. This does **NOT** mean, however, that you can just skip ahead to Mistake #7 and ignore this entire section. Read on to see why.

How to fix it: Often the most difficult part is to estimate or predict future expenses, and since nobody has a crystal ball it's very likely that your estimate will be wrong. You can significantly improve the reliability of your estimate by doing two things: 1) review your past history of spending by looking at your bank and credit card statements, receipts, etc. to see how much you have actually spent on a monthly basis for each of the major expense categories, and 2) consider whether any major changes are likely to happen in the coming months (such as moving, buying or selling a car or big appliance, getting married, having a baby, sending a child to college, retiring, etc.). Predicting new expenses is particularly difficult because you don't have a past record to go by, but you can make your best guess and then double it just in case. You can omit this part if you really hate budgets, but at least look at ball-park figures based on past experience to get an idea of where you'll end up if nothing changes.

Even if you opt not to predict future expenses, you do need to have a way to keep track of your actual spending. There are many software programs that make this easy and accurate by allowing you to download your banking and credit card transactions directly into the software (a great free resource is mint.com), and the program sorts many if not all of them into categories automatically and gives you the totals in an easy-to-read format or graphs. Setting up and using these programs takes very little time, and gives you a wealth of information at your fingertips so you can make smart and informed decisions about your money. Ideally, you would want to review this information monthly or even weekly, though for some people it may be enough to look at it once every three months or so. The important point is to do it; you will have no control without reliable information.

You have no control over your money without reliable information on actual spending.

 Now make it personal: Consider the following questions and record your answers in the space provided or in your Prosperity Notebook.

How are you currently keeping track of your income and expenses?

If you use a software-based system to manage your money, how often do you update and review the information?

If you do not currently use a software-based system, do an online search for "money management software" and choose one. Some common options include Quicken by Intuit, Money by Microsoft, and mint.com.

You can also set up online access for all of your bank and credit card accounts, which most software programs will also require to work properly. This industry is by now very well established and respected, so you can rest assured that your information is safe and private. Which program did you choose?

Now set a timeframe for how often you will update and review your information. Make a regular date and time and record it as an appointment in your calendar. Make it frequent enough that it will take approximately an hour or two at the most to update and review your current situation each time. What timeframe did you choose?

If you would like to set up and use a budget, you can either use your money management software (most offer this feature) or download our spreadsheet template from www.Kimberly-Carlton.com.

MISTAKE #7 – NOT INVESTING IN INCOME-PRODUCING ASSETS

<u>**Why it's important**</u>: Assets do two things: 1) They *create* value (productive assets), and 2) They *preserve* value (passive or non-productive assets). Productive assets <u>produce</u> income. Other examples of productive assets include machinery, land and buildings, dividend-yielding stocks, bonds, and annuities. You can – and should – also think of <u>yourself</u> as a productive asset! Your time, intelligence, skills, knowledge, talents and more can be used productively to create value for yourself, others, or both. If your goal is to increase your income in the relatively short term, seek opportunities to invest in productive assets.

Non-productive assets provide a way to maintain and hopefully even increase the value of what you own, and can be seen as a source of future income when you sell them either for cash or to acquire income-generating productive assets. Some examples of these kinds of assets include gold and other precious metals, a home that you own and live in, diamonds and other precious stones, commodities, stocks, and real estate.

What about cash? "Cash is King" is a phrase we've all heard but what kind of asset is it? The value of cash is its flexibility. Sitting in a bank, cash is a non-productive asset (to you, not to the bank) that tends to lose its value over time, which goes against both of the two principles above defining assets. But the flexibility of cash makes it an ideal buffer against uncertainty and risk, so a smart strategy will trade off the security it can provide against its non-income-producing and –preserving nature. How much of your cash should you invest in income-producing assets and how much should you keep in an emergency fund? The answer depends on your current situation, but an accepted rule of thumb is that you should have enough cash to cover three months' worth of expenses in the event that you lose all of your earned income. When building assets, consider how you want to split your money between short-term and long-term goals based on where you're starting from. Both are important, so be sure to include both and choose what makes you most comfortable between a 50-50 and a 90-10 split (in whichever direction best aligns with your values and needs, given your current situation).

ഓരോ

Investing in assets is an important part of any wealth-building strategy.

ഓരോ

ഓരോ

Assets *create* and *preserve* value.

ഓരോ

How to fix it: Assets are commonly defined as property that you own: your house, cars, rental properties, stocks and bonds, precious metals and stones (e.g., jewelry), even appliances and collectibles. Normally, assets are durable goods – things that last a long time and cannot be "used up" or consumed by anyone. They tend to hold or even increase their value over time, like gold or real estate, though some do lose value ("depreciate") over time, like cars. Keep in mind that assets can also be *intangible*, meaning they can also include things that cannot be touched physically: intellectual property (specialized knowledge, patents, and inventions), reputation, etc.

If income represents a *flow* of money, then assets represent a *source* of income. They exist and are measured at a <u>particular moment</u> in time (you may recall that income is measured over a span of time). A good analogy would be a well: the water that is contained within the well is like an asset, and the amount or value of it can  be measured on any given day (and compared to either measurements taken of the same well on other days or to measurements taken of other wells). Running a pump to bring the water out of the well is similar to income, as the speed and amount of water removed with the pump are measured over time (by the hour or day, for example).

Investing current income in the purchase of assets is an important part of any wealth-building strategy, and you'll want to consider a few key factors in deciding what to invest in. The foremost among these is *risk*. Risk represents the possibility that you might lose all or part of your investment. The purchase of any asset involves a certain amount of risk and normally the level of risk is closely related to the *rate of return on investment (ROI)*. In other words, the safer an investment is, the less you normally earn from it (think of a savings account at your bank, which is insured by the FDIC and pays very little in interest), while riskier investments can have higher payoffs (venture capital invests in start-ups and the few big "hits" more than make up for the losses from all the companies that fail).

There are different ways of calculating ROI, and if you're serious about investing it would be worth your time to learn about this in more detail, but the general idea is that the difference in value between what you put in and what you get out of a deal can be divided by the amount of investment to reveal the rate of return. For example, if you invest $100 in the stock market and your investment is worth $112 in one year, then your rate of return is:

> **Assets** are property that you own.

$$\frac{(\text{Ending value} - \text{beginning value})}{\text{Beginning value}} = \text{Rate of return}$$

$$\frac{(112 - 100)}{100} = 0.12\ (12\%)$$

To get the percent, just multiply the final result by 100 (.12 x 100 = 12).

You can use the same principle to figure out your cash rate of return by comparing your cash investment with your cash payoff (this can make sense when you invest in ways that also require taking on debt). For example, let's say you buy a house for $55,000 and you sell it in one year for $70,000. To buy the house, you pay 10% down ($5,500) and finance the rest ($49,500). Here is how you would calculate your overall rate of return:

$$\frac{(\text{Ending value} - (\text{your down payment} + \text{bank financing}))}{\text{Beginning value}} = \text{Rate of return}$$

$$\frac{(70,000 - (5,500 + 49,500))}{55,000} = 0.273 \ (27.3\%)$$

$$\frac{(70,000 - 55,000)}{55,000} = 0.273 \ (27.3\%)$$

This rate of return would be accurate if you had paid cash for the purchase without borrowing. On a cash basis, however, you put in $5,500 (10% of $55,000) and your profit (ending value of $70,000 – beginning value of $55,000) was $15,000 <u>after repaying your cash down payment</u>, or:

$$\frac{(\text{Your profit or loss} - \text{your down payment})}{\text{Your down payment}} = \text{Cash rate of return}$$

$$\frac{(15,000 - 5,500)}{5,500} = 1.727 \ (172.7\%)$$

Notice that 100% return means that you've doubled your investment, or earned as much extra as the original amount you put in. So a 172.7% return means that your original investment was paid back in full PLUS you received almost twice that amount in addition to that original investment!

This simple example shows the power of *leverage*, which is simply another way of saying you use other people's money (OPM) to your own advantage. Many people have used this tool as a way to enrich themselves, and it can be powerful. However, *beware!* Leverage is like a magnifying glass – it can help you increase your earnings, and it can also burn you because it works in both directions. Let's flip our example around to demonstrate. You purchase a house for $55,000 and in one year, it's worth $40,000. Your overall rate of return, assuming you paid cash for the house, would be:

$$\frac{(\text{Ending value} - \text{beginning value})}{\text{Beginning value}} = \text{Rate of return}$$

$$\frac{(40,000 - 55,000)}{55,000} = -0.273 \ (-27.3\% \text{ which is a LOSS!})$$

On the cash value, it would look different. In this case, your "profit" represents the amount you still owe to the bank that your $40,000 sale price didn't cover, or $40,000 - $49,500 = - $9,500. (Note that your total loss is $15,000 = your original cash investment + what you still owe the bank.)

$$\frac{(\text{Your profit or loss} - \text{your down payment})}{\text{Your down payment}} = \text{Cash rate of return}$$

$$\frac{(-9,500 - 5,500)}{5,500} = -2.727 \ (-272.7\%)$$

Here, notice that a MINUS 100% return (-100%) means that you lost everything you put in. So, a -272.7% return means that you lost your original investment PLUS almost twice as much extra in addition to what you put in!

This brings us back to the issue of risk. Any time you buy an investment, there is *always* a risk that you might lose part or all of what you invest. Some investments have little or no risk, and these investments virtually always have *low* rates of return. A rule of thumb is, **if an investment has a high rate of return, it also comes with a high risk of loss**. If someone selling you an investment claims otherwise, do two things: 1) insist that they prove to you in clear and simple language how the investment works (get it *in writing*), and 2) get a second (and even third!) opinion from someone you trust who is NOT likely to benefit from your purchase of this asset.

Risk management itself is a subject it would be worth your time to learn more about if you are serious about building wealth, but here the last point to make on the subject is that one of the key strategies for reducing risk in investments is to *diversify* – ensure that you own a variety of types of assets. Simply put, do not put all of your eggs in one basket! Just as you will benefit significantly from receiving income from many different kinds of sources, both active and passive, you must invest in different kinds of assets to produce that income.

A high rate of return also comes with a high risk of loss.

 Now make it personal: Consider the following questions and record your answers in the space provided or in your Prosperity Notebook.

List the productive (income-generating) assets you currently own and the amount of income they contribute. Form 7-1:

Productive Asset	Income Per Month	Income Per Year
Totals		

List the non-productive (value-preserving) assets you currently own and their values at time of purchase and currently. Calculate the Return on Investment to date for each based on current value relative to purchase price [((Current value – Purchase price) / Purchase price) x 100]. Form 7-2:

Non-Productive Asset	Purchase Price	Current Value	ROI (%)
Example: Stock portfolio	$1,000.00	$1,200.00	20.00%
Totals	$1,000.00	$1,200.00	20.00%

Evaluate the extent to which your assets are diversified (and your risks minimized) by filling in the following table. Asset types are listed from those that typically have lower risk of loss to those with higher risk, but keep in mind that you're not necessarily better off having most of your assets held in lower-risk categories. How to spread out your asset holdings is called *asset allocation* and there is no "one-size-fits-all" formula that determines what's best for you. This is an important decision and it is best made by you and a professional financial planner based on your specific situation and goals.

Form 7-3:

Asset Type	Amount Invested	% of Total Investments
Cash (including savings and money market accounts)		
Government bonds		
CDs and annuities		
Foreign currency		
Real estate and REITs		
Precious metals		
Collectibles (art, wine, autos, etc.)		
Corporate bonds		
Stocks and mutual funds		
Foreign stocks and investments		
Totals		

Tip: Resist the temptation to buy assets that everybody else is buying. A bubble *is said to exist when prices are over-inflated due to abnormally strong demand. Remember that past performance is NOT a reliable predictor of future performance. If you really want to invest in something that's currently in high demand, be sure to take the time to learn in detail about the asset type, what factors affect its value, and how to recognize a truly good deal. A general rule of thumb is to buy when everybody else is* selling *and to sell when everybody else is* buying.

MISTAKE #8 – TAKING ON EXCESSIVE CONSUMER DEBT

Why it's important: Debt can be seen as a necessary evil because although many people have a natural aversion to owing money to others, the power of leverage it provides can make a significant difference in how quickly you can accumulate assets and, therefore, wealth. Used properly, this very sharp tool can greatly improve your financial well-being and, conversely, when used recklessly it can cause great damage.

ഋരൔ

Debt provides *leverage*, which magnifies both gains _and_ losses.

ഋരൔ

The fact that credit has become much easier to access is both good and bad. It used to be that "only people who already have money can borrow money" and this meant that the power of leverage was only available to the relatively wealthiest among us, so the road to riches was longer and harder for those who were poorer. In that sense it's good that more people have access to this important tool. However, the negative consequence is that since leverage cuts in both directions, people with less to lose can end up much <u>worse</u> off than they started.

The other problem is that such easy access to credit also makes it easy for people to fail to consider <u>how</u> they are using this sharp and powerful tool – is it to purchase assets, which would generate the additional income necessary to more than cover the additional expense of the debt obligation, or is it to purchase consumables that will be used up today and provide no future value? To make it clear, think of prosperity as a cliff with you at the bottom with no way to climb and your only tool is a shovel (leverage). You dig up a shovelful of dirt and use it to build a staircase up the side of the cliff. With each shovelful, the hole (debt) gets bigger, but so does the staircase (asset). Using debt this way, you can reach prosperity. However, if you throw the dirt into the wind, you will just end up in a deep hole of debt with no way to get out. That's what happens when you use credit to buy things that get used up today and provide no future value.

How to fix it: Debt (aka *liabilities*) is defined as what you owe to others – whether to individuals (such as relatives or friends) or to institutions (banks or credit unions). Consumer debt really became common after WWII and is one reason why the middle class grew in size and prosperity during that time. By the end of 2009, U.S. consumer debt (excluding mortgage debt) was nearly $2.5 trillion, with the average homeowner spending about 17% of disposable (after-tax) income on debt payments (including mortgages) and the average renter spending close to 25% of disposable income on debt payments.

The simplest way to think of debt is as a promise to pay later for what you buy today. As we saw in the previous section, debt (aka OPM or "other people's money") provides *leverage*, which means it can allow you to earn AND lose considerably more than the actual cash you have of your own to put toward any given purchase.

Keep in mind that while expenses, like income, are best thought of as flows of money, debt is like assets in that it represents a source or cause – only where assets are a source of income or cash inflow, debt is a source of expenses or cash outflow.

> *Debt* (aka *liabilities*) is what you owe to others.

Getting out of debt requires focus and discipline (the key benefits a budget provides, as discussed in Mistake #6). Remember, though, that debt itself is not necessarily a problem. Debt is a problem when it is excessive, which can mean either that the amount owed is so high you can't afford the payments or that the interest rate is so high you end up paying way more for something than it's actually worth. Debt is also a problem when you use it foolishly, such as for purchases of things you can't afford and don't really need. On the other hand, debt can be a real benefit when it is used to purchase assets that will produce income for you in the future.

 Now make it personal: Consider the following questions and record your answers in the space provided or in your Prosperity Notebook.

List all of the debts you owe, the amount of each, and whether each represents the purchase of an asset that either produces income or preserves value.

Debt	Amount	Used for asset? (Y/N)
Mortgage on own home		
Mortgage on rental properties		
Car loans		
All credit cards combined		
Business loans		
HELOC (Home Equity Line of Credit)		
Personal loans		
Other:		
Other:		
Other:		
Totals		

Based on the above, what percentage of your debt is an investment in an asset?   %

What percentage was "dirt on the wind?"   %

List your total credit card debt by account along with the amounts owed and current interest rate.

Card/Account	Amount Owed	Interest Rate (%)
Totals		

Ideally, no one would use credit to pay for current living expenses (paying later to consume now) instead of current income, yet it often happens and it is sometimes necessary. Given your personal situation right now, what would you need to do to reduce the "dirt on the wind" percentage to zero – or as close to it as is realistic for you now – within the next 90 days? List 3-5 things that would make a real difference.

1.
2.
3.
4.
5.

Are you willing to commit to do these things? If not, why not?

CHARTING YOUR COURSE

Now it's time to pull together everything you've done into a simple and clear "roadmap" of where you want to be and how you will get there. As with any journey, you need two things: 1) a destination that is clear and compelling to you, and 2) specific, concrete actions that bring you closer to your destination step by step. No one can do it for you; you must commit to leading the way for yourself and taking the actions on a regular basis that will move you toward your goals.

Fear and doubt are the biggest obstacles to success. These two monsters can show up in many ways to block and even sabotage your dreams, and you will need a strategy for disabling them. Many times people are stopped in their tracks by fear or doubt before they even get started! If you have thoughts like, "This is just too hard, I can't possibly do it," or "This will never work, so why even bother," then you know what I'm talking about.

ঙি০৪

"Whether you think you can, or whether you think you can't, you're right." Henry Ford

ঙিও৪

Are you your own biggest fan and supporter, or your own worst critic? Unfortunately, most people are far more critical than supportive of themselves, and this seriously limits their ability to achieve their goals and dreams. Yet, successful people believe in themselves and consciously reinforce that positive message by surrounding themselves with others who inspire, uplift, and motivate them to persist in the pursuit of their goals.

So if you want to succeed in taking control of your money, you will benefit tremendously from doing the following to help you stay focused and motivated:

- Spending 5-10 minutes every day imagining in vivid detail how fantastic you will feel when you've achieved your goals;

- Practicing positive self-talk every day ("I know I can do this!" and "I feel so good about myself for taking control over my money!" for example);

- Supporting yourself by reading, listening to, and watching inspirational material; and

- Enlisting the help and support of 2-3 people you trust who love you and want you to succeed.

NOT doing these things is the same as setting yourself up for failure.

Here is a very simple and effective process that will help you distill everything you've learned into a practical plan that will lead you toward the fulfillment of your goals.

1. Set up a support system for yourself. This is essential to help you stay motivated and moving forward. A good support system provides two essential ingredients for success: encouragement and accountability.

2. Refine and clarify your long-term goals. You should have a crystal clear picture in your head of where you are going and why it's important to you. Without this, you risk simply drifting aimlessly to nowhere in particular.

3. Set short-term targets that are en route to your desired destination. You need to have a sense of how you're going to get from where you are to where you want to be. Otherwise, you're likely to find yourself stuck in place, spinning your wheels.

4. Specify the concrete actions you will take to reach your targets. Don't worry if you don't have all the details sorted out – the essential point here is to take those first few steps and get moving! As you move forward, the logical next steps will come more clearly into focus.

5. **Act!** DO something. The best-laid plans in the world are worthless if you don't act on them. Even if you devote only 15 minutes a day to actions that move you toward your goals, you will start to build momentum.

 Now make it personal: Consider the following questions and record your answers in the space provided or in your Prosperity Notebook.

Describe your support system. Who is cheering you on? How often do you check in with progress reports and status updates? How does your support team hold you accountable? What can you do to make it even more effective for you?

Name at least one person who you will check in with at least once per month (we'll call them your Money Mentor). This needs to be someone you can trust to share your financial goals with, give updates on your progress, and who will actively support and encourage you. Ideally, it will also be someone you can call on a moment's notice when you're feeling discouraged, when you need someone to help talk you out of a purchase that doesn't support your goals, when you just have to share your excitement about a recent victory, etc. To be clear, you will NOT

Tip: Look for someone who can (and will!) unconditionally support and encourage you. In a sense, you are trusting this person with your life! Choose well.

ask these people for money. The more people (within reason!) you can turn to, the better. List their names here.

Now call each person whose name you just wrote and explicitly request their help as described above. Tell them that you are working to take control of your money, and you'd like to share your goals with them, ask their advice and help as needed, and celebrate your achievements with them. If you don't get an enthusiastic, unequivocal agreement, it may be best to thank them and reconsider whether this is really the right person to rely on. If you have one enthusiastic supporter, you're probably better off with just that one than with 2 or 3 lackluster ones. List the name(s) of your Money Mentor here.

Working backward from the "Now Make It Personal" sections from Mistake #3 to Mistake #1, review your answers as you wrote them in this workbook or your Prosperity Notebook. Now write (either revised or simply restated) your top 3 long-term (5-year) SMART goals. As before, use the present tense.

1.
2.
3.

Translate each 5-year goal you just wrote into a 1-year goal.

1.
2.
3.

Complete your personal Declaration of Financial Freedom on the next page.

DECLARATION OF FINANCIAL FREEDOM			
5-Year Goals			
On (date), I:			
1.	2.	3.	4.
1-Year Goals			
On (date), I:			
1.	2.	3.	4.
3-Month Targets			
Income	Expenses	Assets	Debts
1.	1.	1.	1.
2.	2.	2.	2.
3.	3.	3.	3.
3-Month Action Plan			
Income	Expenses	Assets	Debts
1.	1.	1.	1.
2.	2.	2.	2.
3.	3.	3.	3.

STAYING ON COURSE

Congratulations! If you have been doing the exercises in the previous sections, you are well on your way to success. In fact, you're already halfway there. You have taken a deep look at your financial hopes and values, set clear and specific goals that are consistent with your hopes and values, shared your intentions for a more prosperous future with others who care about your success, made a plan for how you'll gain control over your money, and taken the first steps toward making it all real. You're not done yet, but you've accomplished a lot and that's something to be proud of!

ဆာ

You're halfway there... but the most important part lies ahead!

ဆာ

Staying On Course may be the most important of all – especially for those of us who have a tendency to get all fired up and excited about something only to find our enthusiasm and commitment decline over time. If you've ever made a New Year's resolution that you gave up on by February or joined a gym that you stopped paying the monthly membership fees for only long after you last saw the inside of the building, you already know that maintaining a sustained commitment to change is <u>hard</u>.

It turns out that the reason why change can be so difficult to maintain has a lot to do with how the brain works. The first point to understand is that you can stop beating yourself up for stumbling and even getting stuck somewhere short of success – it's not a character defect, or proof of laziness or incompetence on your part. The second point is to realize that you're not helpless, because once you understand how the brain actually works you can begin to work with, rather than against, its natural tendencies.

The details are well beyond the scope of this workbook and they are well documented and described elsewhere (check out *The Answer* by J. Assaraf and M. Smith for a very readable explanation, some highlights of which are offered below). The key points to keep in mind are these:

- Each of us has a "conscious" and "nonconscious" aspect to our brains. The conscious mind is the source of intention – thinking, reasoning, analyzing, learning, observing and concentrating are all functions of this part of the brain. Will, memory, perception, intuition, and imagination also reside here. This is the part of your brain you use when you make decisions about how you want your life to be and what changes you'd like to make. Here's the rub, though: the conscious mind only controls about **2-4%** of perception and behavior.

- The nonconscious mind is the true powerhouse. Not only does it monitor, manage and maintain the many biological functions required to keep the body alive, it also keeps track of every experience you've ever had and automates most of your activities – the source of the power of habits. It controls the vast majority of behavior and perception (96-98%) and operates at lightning speed (processing about 400 billion bits of information per second, in contrast to the 2,000 bits per second processed by the conscious mind).

- Habits and beliefs form the core of the nonconscious mind's "programming." On average, most of us have heard "no, you can't" about 30 times more often than "yes, you can." The nonconscious mind forgets nothing, and it acts in accordance with what it's been taught. This is why *what you believe to be true* has such power – the habit formed from repetition is thousands of times stronger than your new desire. Thousands of times stronger.

- Setting goals is a function of the conscious mind. Achieving them is a function of the nonconscious mind. This is why it is so important to take an active role in programming your brain through meditation, daily positive self-talk, reading/watching/listening to motivational materials, etc. Developing new habits takes work – conscious, active, repetitive work. You use your force of will and discipline (under the control of the conscious mind) until the activity becomes second nature (under the control of the nonconscious mind).

 Now make it personal: Consider the following questions and record your answers in the space provided or in your Prosperity Notebook.

Think back to a time in your life when you wanted something so badly you were willing to do just about anything to get it, and then did succeed in getting it. What helped you stay motivated and on track?

Now close your eyes and consider the financial goals you've set for yourself. How intense is your desire for these things compared to the example from an earlier time you just thought about? What if you fail to achieve these goals – is that an outcome you're prepared to accept?

Hopefully, the goals you set are so meaningful and close to your heart that your answer to the previous question was something along the lines of, "failure is not an option!" If you answered any other way than that, then go back and look at your goals again. If you don't feel passionately committed to them, then they aren't the right goals for you. Perhaps they're someone else's goals or hopes for you, or a reflection of something you think you should want but deep down really don't, or maybe they're either too ambitious or not ambitious enough at this point in your life. Rewrite them, as many times as it takes until you feel a fire inside of you that will not allow you to accept failure as an option.

If you ARE ready to declare that failure is not an option, hooray for you!! Really, this is what will propel you to success. Success in anything requires 3 things: *belief* that you can do it, *commitment* to do what it takes, and *skills/knowledge* relevant to what you're trying to accomplish. By far, the first two ingredients outweigh the last in importance. If you're fired up about your goals, it's a good sign that you believe in them. Now it's time for commitment, for you to declare your willingness to do what it takes to achieve them. Get your personal Declaration of Financial Freedom from last section and in the space provided at the bottom, copy in your own writing the following statement and then sign your name and put the date next to it: "I accept 100% complete responsibility for my financial situation,

Be firm in your goals, but flexible in your strategies for reaching them!

without exception or condition. As of now, I am taking full control over my thoughts, words, and actions. I use my money joyfully in the service of the goals stated above." Make several copies of this document and put them in places where you'll see them throughout your day – on a wall in your office, your desk, your purse or briefcase, your car, your bathroom wall, wherever you'll see them. To make it even more powerful, make the copies <u>before</u> writing the statement above and write it, by hand, on each copy individually. Why? Because the act of writing imprints the commitment in your nonconscious mind, and your handwriting personalizes each copy so that your brain is less likely to tune it out as "another one of the same…"

Choose a specific time when you will review your Declaration each day. Put it in your calendar as a recurring (daily) appointment (10 minutes is enough time).

Now choose one date every month when you will review your current financial situation. It could be a pay day, the date when the last credit card statement for the previous month comes in, the day of your birth, or any other date that is meaningful to you. Put it in your calendar as a recurring (monthly) appointment. Give yourself a full hour. Use the time to:

1. Review the balances for all your accounts (checking, savings, credit cards, etc.) and compare them to the previous month. Where do you see improvements? Where don't you see them? What's the net effect – are you better off overall than last month? If not, figure out why (some changes take more time than others, and external circumstances certainly play a role). If yes, celebrate! (Not by spending money! Be creative and reward yourself with something meaningful that does NOT cost money.)

2. Now review your Declaration of Financial Freedom. Look at your 3-month targets and see how much progress you've made toward them. Are you ahead of schedule? Not as far as you'd hoped to be? If you need to, revise your goals.

3. Review your 3-month Action Plan in your Declaration. Check off actions that you've completed (you can cross them off, put a star next to them, whatever makes you feel good about getting it done!), decide if the ones remaining need to be revised, and add any new actions that come to mind.

Remember, as you move forward on your path you will encounter new information, ideas, feedback from previous actions, etc. Be firm in your goals, but flexible in your strategies for reaching them!

4. Call your Money Mentor and share your insights. Ask for feedback and advice if you like.

Choose a date every quarter (3 months) when you will review your progress toward your larger goals. Obvious choices would be early April, early July, early October, and early January, but you can set them for whenever works best for you. Pick a specific date (e.g., the 5th) and put it in your calendar as an appointment that recurs every 3 months. Give yourself 1-2 hours. This can coincide with your monthly appointment – in which case you might only need an additional 30 minutes. Use the time to:

1. Review your Declaration and determine where you stand on each of your 3-month targets. Since you've already been keeping on top of them each month, you should quickly see whether you've achieved them. Make a list of all that you've accomplished in the past three months, whether or not you had originally listed them as goals or targets. Spend a full 10 minutes simply feeling pleased and proud of yourself – don't skip this! Allow a feeling of gratitude to wash over you, and bask in it. Remind yourself of why your goals are so important to you, how amazing it feels to accomplish them, and experience the pleasure of success NOW for the progress you've made so far. Set a timer for 10 minutes and use ALL of that time to praise yourself and experience gratitude for where you are.

2. Create a new Declaration of Financial Freedom, copying your long-term (5-year and 1-year) goals onto it. If you feel inspired to update your long-term goals, do so. Set new 3-month targets. Write out your new 3-month action plan.

3. Make copies, then handwrite your commitment at the bottom ("I accept 100% complete responsibility for my financial situation, without exception or condition. As of now, I am taking full control over my thoughts, words, and actions. I use my money joyfully in the service of the goals stated above.") of each and put them in the places you've chosen.

4. Check in with your Money Mentor (MM) and share what you've accomplished and your new goals. Ideally, give a copy of your Declaration to your MM. Again, ask for support in whatever form is most helpful to you. And, don't forget to share your gratitude with your MM! This might be a great time to take them out for a cup of coffee or invite them for dinner at your house. Celebrate your successes together! The more your MM feels appreciated and a part of your success, the more willingly they're likely to continue to help you.

Choose a 1-year and 5-year anniversary date when you will review your progress and celebrate your successes. Put them in your calendar.

CONGRATULATIONS! You are well on your way to being the master of your money! I hope you have found this workbook helpful, and I would love to hear your thoughts on what you found most useful as well as any ideas you might have for how to improve it. Please leave comments or suggestions at www.Kimberly-Carlton.com and HAPPY SAILING!

42

Selected Bibliography

Lynne Twist, *The Soul of Money*

Mark V. Hansen & Robert G. Allen, *Cash in a Flash*

David Wood, *Get Paid for Who You Are*

John Assaraf and Murray Smith, *The Answer*

ABOUT THE AUTHOR

Kimberly Carlton is a lifelong seeker and student of love and spiritual growth. She has devoted her career to educating and supporting people who are committed to controlling their own destiny. As a nonprofit executive and entrepreneurship educator, she has taught thousands of people how to improve their lives financially. A graduate of Pomona College and the Stanford Graduate School of Business, she is passionate about encouraging people to follow their dreams.

www.ingramcontent.com/pod-product-compliance
Lightning Source LLC
Chambersburg PA
CBHW050825180526
45159CB00004B/1786